The AI Dissertation Advantage: Strategic Prompts to Fast-Track Your Research, Writing, and Defense

Robert O. Hassell, ED.D.

BK Royston Publishing
Jeffersonville, IN 47131

Copyright© 2025

All Rights Reserved. No part of this book may be reproduced, stored in a retrieval system, or transmitted by any means without the written permission of the author.

Cover Design: Hassell Enterprises

ISBN: 978-1-967282-69-2

Printed in the United States of America

A Heartfelt Dedication

To
Dr. Robbie K. Melton
and
Dr. Deborah Chisom

In recognition of extraordinary leadership, unwavering guidance, steadfast support, and the courage to push boundaries

---

In the ever-evolving landscape of higher education and technology, there are rare individuals who not only navigate change but create it, shape it, and inspire others to embrace it. Dr. Robbie K. Melton and Dr. Deborah Chisom are two such extraordinary leaders whose vision, dedication, and relentless pursuit of excellence have transformed countless lives and institutions.

Dr. Robbie K. Melton, your journey as Provost and Vice President for Technology & Innovation at Tennessee State University exemplifies what it means to be a true pioneer. Your groundbreaking work in the Internet of Everything (IoE) and smart mobile technologies has not only advanced academic discourse but has opened new pathways for learning that transcend traditional boundaries. From the halls of Tennessee State University to the villages of Malawi, Africa, where you serve as UNICEF Teacher Education Technology Trainer, your impact knows no borders.

Your remarkable achievements—speak to a career dedicated not to personal glory, but to lifting others. Your role as an "Appologist" has revolutionized how we think about mobile learning, making education accessible even in environments with limited internet and power. You've shown us that innovation isn't just about having the latest technology; it's about finding creative solutions that serve humanity.

Dr. Deborah Chisom, your embodiment of the "True Blue TSU" spirit through four degrees from Tennessee State University demonstrates an unwavering commitment to growth and excellence. As Assistant Vice President at the Avon Williams Off-Campus Site, you've created bridges—connecting students to opportunities through Academic eSports, making education more accessible through Open Educational Resources (OER), fostering community through the eTiger

Podcast, and strengthening alumni bonds through TSU Alumni Connect.

Your passion for helping students reach their full potential resonates in everything you do. Like Malcolm X's powerful words that guide you— *"Education is the passport to the future, for tomorrow belongs to those who prepare for it today"*—you understand that education is not just about imparting knowledge, but about preparing minds and hearts for the challenges and opportunities that lie ahead.

Together, you both represent the very best of educational leadership. Your guidance has been a beacon for those navigating uncertain waters, your support has been the foundation upon which dreams are built, and your gentle but persistent push has helped so many discover strengths they never knew they possessed. You've shown us that true leadership isn't about commanding from the top, but about walking alongside others, lifting them up, and empowering them to soar.

In a world that often celebrates individual achievement, you both have demonstrated that the greatest success comes from the success of others. Your collaborative spirit, your commitment to innovation, and your deep care for students and colleagues alike have created ripple effects that will be felt for generations to come.

Thank you for your vision that sees beyond the present to imagine what could be. Thank you for your courage to challenge the status quo and push boundaries that others might have thought immovable. Thank you for your patience in nurturing growth, even when progress seemed slow. Thank you for your wisdom in knowing when to guide gently and when to push firmly. And thank you for your hearts that never forgot that behind every innovation, every program, every initiative, are real people with real dreams and real potential.

Your leadership has not just advanced institutions; it has transformed lives. Your guidance has not just provided direction; it has instilled confidence. Your support has not just offered assistance; it has created community. And your push has not just motivated action; it has inspired excellence.

As you continue to shape the future of education and technology, know that your impact extends far beyond what can be measured in awards or accolades. You have planted seeds of possibility, nurtured gardens of growth, and created forests of opportunity that will continue to flourish long after your direct involvement.

With deepest gratitude, profound respect, and heartfelt appreciation for all you have done, all you continue to do, and all you inspire others to become.

"The influence of a great teacher extends beyond the classroom, beyond the campus, and beyond the years—it lives forever in the lives they have touched."

Humbly Submitted,

Robert O. Hassell, Ed.D.

Transforming Academic Writing in Higher Education: An Ethical Framework for Artificial Intelligence Integration Through Prompting Excellence and Progressive Learning

Abstract

The integration of artificial intelligence (AI) in higher education academic writing represents a paradigmatic shift that, when implemented ethically and strategically, can significantly enhance learning outcomes while maintaining academic integrity. This manual examines the critical role of effective prompting in AI-assisted academic writing, utilizing Dr. Robbie K. Melton's AI-Prompt Scale Rubric, Dr. Nicole Arrighi's Five-Stage Learning Spectrum and Mr. Marcus Horton's P.A.C. It Up as foundational frameworks.

The academic prompts presented for dissertations, thesis writing, and IRB processes are developed using the comprehensive ASCEND-AI framework, which integrates key elements from the AI-Prompt Scale Rubric, Arrighi AI-C2 Utilization Spectrum, Bloom's Taxonomy, and ISTE Standards. This integrated approach provides educators with pedagogically sound tools for designing AI learning experiences that support progressive skill development, evaluate prompt quality across multiple dimensions, and align practices with established educational models.

By transitioning students from convenience-based AI usage to competence-driven applications through structured prompting strategies, institutions can prepare learners for the digital workforce while preserving the fundamental values of academic excellence and intellectual honesty. The framework demonstrates how AI prompts can promote various levels of cognitive engagement and develop essential AI literacy skills required for contemporary academic and professional success.

Keywords: artificial intelligence, academic writing, prompting, higher education, academic integrity, digital literacy, ASCEND-AI framework, dissertation writing, thesis development

Table of Contents

Dedication	iii
Abstract	ix
Introduction	xiii
Chapter 1 75 General AI Prompts for Topic Exploration, Research and Analysis	1
Chapter 2 75 Dissertation Research AI Prompts for Literature Reviews, Methodologies, Introductions, and Future Research	17
Chapter 3 75 Dissertation Research AI Prompts Based on AQR Academic Quality Review Checklist	37
Chapter 4 75 Dissertation Research AI Prompts Tennessee State University Specific Requirements Formatting and Style Compliance	59
Chapter 5 75 IRB Process AI Prompts	85
Conclusion	107
References	109

AI Integration in Higher Education: A Framework for Academic Writing Enhancement

Introduction

Higher education institutions face a pivotal moment where artificial intelligence technologies converge with traditional academic values of scholarly excellence and intellectual integrity. Educational leaders must determine how to leverage AI capabilities for learning enhancement while maintaining critical thinking, originality, and academic rigor. Advanced AI language models present both remarkable opportunities and substantial challenges for academia, requiring institutions to develop comprehensive frameworks that guide ethical and effective integration into academic writing processes.

The transformation of academic writing through AI integration necessitates a fundamental reconceptualization of teaching, learning, and assessment methodologies. Rather than perceiving AI as threatening academic integrity, institutions must recognize it as a powerful instrument that, through proper guidance via effective prompting strategies and progressive learning frameworks, can enhance cognitive engagement and strengthen critical thinking. This approach requires systematic implementation of pedagogically sound methodologies that preserve academic rigor while preparing students for professional environments where AI literacy becomes increasingly vital.

Tennessee State University has emerged as a leader in this transformative approach through the development of comprehensive AI integration frameworks. The ASCEND-AI framework provides educators with pedagogically sound tools for designing AI learning experiences that support progressive skill development and evaluate prompt quality across multiple dimensions (Hassell, 2024). Complementing this approach, the P.A.C. it up! Educational Aid methodology offers structured guidance for implementing AI tools in educational settings while maintaining pedagogical integrity (Horton, 2024).

Central to effective AI integration is the recognition that prompting excellence serves as the foundation for meaningful educational outcomes. Melton's (2023) AI-Prompt Scale framework establishes comprehensive evaluation criteria for developing prompts that maximize educational value while preserving academic integrity. This framework, combined with Arrighi's (2023) Five-Stage Learning Spectrum, creates a robust foundation for transitioning students from convenience-based AI usage to competence-driven applications.

The integration of these frameworks addresses the critical need for systematic approaches to AI implementation in higher education. By establishing clear guidelines for ethical AI use, institutions can maintain academic standards while leveraging technology's potential to enhance learning outcomes. This approach recognizes that success depends not on AI avoidance, but on creating structured pathways that guide students through progressive skill development stages, ensuring they develop both technical proficiency and critical thinking capabilities essential for academic and professional success.

Progressive Learning Approach: From Convenience to Competence

The Arrighi AI-C2 Utilization Spectrum

The Five-Stage Learning Spectrum for Utilizing Artificial Intelligence in Education provides a developmental framework that guides students from passive AI consumption to autonomous innovation (Arrighi, 2023). This "Convenience to Competence" (C2) progression offers a roadmap for ethical AI integration that preserves academic integrity while enhancing learning outcomes.

Stage 1: Passive Consumer (Convenience) represents the entry level where students use AI for basic information retrieval and simple question-answering. While offering limited cognitive enrichment, this stage provides important foundation building for AI tool familiarity and developing basic usage confidence (Arrighi, 2023).

Stage 2: Active Inquirer (Exploration) marks the beginning of more sophisticated AI engagement, where students explore AI functionalities beyond basic tasks through simulations, interactive tutorials, and personalized learning recommendations. This stage represents a crucial transition from convenience-based usage to more educationally meaningful applications (Arrighi, 2023).

Stage 3: Critical Evaluator (Analysis) develops students' abilities to assess AI-generated content critically, compare outputs with credible sources, and understand AI limitations and biases. This stage proves particularly crucial for academic writing, ensuring students maintain analytical skills necessary for scholarly work (Arrighi, 2023).

Stage 4: Collaborative Creator (Application) transforms students into active AI partners, using these tools to create original content, solve complex problems, and explore sophisticated concepts. In academic writing contexts, this stage enables students to leverage AI for research enhancement, argument development, and creative exploration while maintaining their own intellectual contributions (Arrighi, 2023).

Stage 5: Autonomous Innovator (Mastery) represents the highest level of AI literacy, where students become self-directed in their learning journey, using AI to explore novel research avenues and potentially develop their own AI-enhanced learning approaches (Arrighi, 2023).

Cognitive Enhancement Through Progressive Engagement

Progression through the five-stage spectrum facilitates increasing levels of cognitive enrichment while building self-efficacy in AI use (Arrighi, 2023). This developmental approach ensures students don't become dependent on AI for basic thinking processes, but rather learn to use these tools for cognitive capability augmentation and enhancement. In academic writing contexts, this progression enables students to advance from simple information gathering to sophisticated analysis, synthesis, and original contribution.

The framework's emphasis on both cognitive enrichment and self-efficacy addresses two critical concerns in AI-enhanced education: maintaining academic rigor and building student confidence

(Arrighi, 2023). As students progress through the stages, they develop not only technical AI usage skills but also critical thinking abilities necessary to evaluate, synthesize, and build upon AI-generated content.

Integration with ASCEND-AI Framework

The progressive learning approach aligns with the ASCEND-AI framework, which provides educators with pedagogically sound tools for designing AI learning experiences that support progressive skill development (Hassell, 2024). This integrated approach evaluates prompt quality across multiple dimensions and aligns practices with established educational models, ensuring that AI integration enhances rather than replaces fundamental academic skills.

The P.A.C. it up! Educational Aid methodology further supports this progressive approach by providing structured guidance for implementing AI tools in educational settings while maintaining pedagogical integrity (Horton, 2024). Together with Melton's (2023) AI-PromptScale framework, these resources create a comprehensive support system for ethical AI integration in academic writing.

The Critical Foundation: Prompting Excellence and Academic Integrity

The development of academically sound prompts represents a fundamental skill that determines the educational value and ethical implementation of AI in higher education. Melton's (2023) AI-PromptScale framework establishes the critical foundation for this skill development through its comprehensive eight-dimensional evaluation system that encompasses language clarity, curriculum alignment, cognitive engagement, personalization, learning enhancement, applied learning application, accessibility and inclusivity, and ethical considerations. This framework transforms prompting from a simple technical task into a sophisticated pedagogical practice that requires students to articulate their thinking processes, define research parameters, and specify analytical approaches with precision and academic rigor.

The significance of the AI-PromptScale framework extends beyond technical proficiency to encompass metacognitive development and critical thinking enhancement. When students engage with this structured approach to prompt development, they must demonstrate deeper understanding of both subject matter and writing processes, effectively bridging the gap between learning objectives and AI capabilities (Melton,

2023). This process inherently develops critical thinking skills as students must consider multiple perspectives, evaluate source credibility, and synthesize complex information while ensuring their prompts align with specific curricular goals and academic standards.

Complementing this foundation, the P.A.C. it up! Educational Aid methodology provides essential scaffolding for implementing AI tools while maintaining pedagogical integrity (Horton, 2024). This structured approach ensures that AI integration serves educational enhancement rather than academic substitution, guiding students through systematic processes that preserve intellectual rigor while leveraging technological capabilities. The methodology's emphasis on structured implementation creates clear pathways for students to develop competency in AI use while maintaining adherence to academic integrity standards.

The priority nature of teaching academically sound prompt development cannot be overstated, as this skill serves as the primary mechanism for ensuring AI tools enhance rather than compromise academic integrity. Students who master effective prompting techniques learn to use AI as sophisticated instruments for cognitive augmentation rather than intellectual replacement. This mastery requires understanding how to craft prompts that demand critical analysis, synthesis, and original thinking while maintaining transparency and proper attribution in accordance with institutional policies and academic standards.

Furthermore, the integration of these frameworks addresses the urgent need for systematic approaches to AI literacy that prepare students for professional environments where prompt engineering becomes an essential workforce skill. The ability to develop effective prompts that align with academic and professional standards represents a critical competency that extends far beyond the classroom, positioning graduates for success in increasingly AI-integrated professional contexts while ensuring they maintain ethical standards and intellectual integrity throughout their careers.

Tennessee State University's AI Policy Framework: A Pioneering Model for Institutional Development

Tennessee State University's Policy on Responsible Use of Artificial Intelligence (Policy No. 1.09) represents a comprehensive institutional framework that addresses the emerging demands of AI technology integration in higher education. This policy demonstrates how universities can balance innovation with academic integrity while providing clear guidance for all stakeholders.

Policy Framework Analysis
Comprehensive Scope and Stakeholder Coverage

TSU's policy applies universally to "faculty, staff, students, and employees who use AI tools for academic, research, or administrative purposes," ensuring institutional-wide consistency while recognizing diverse use cases across different university functions.

Multi-Tiered Governance Structure

The policy establishes clear oversight through three responsible offices:

- **Office of Academic Affairs**: Academic policy implementation

- **Office of Technology Services (OTS)**: Technical security and data protection

- **Office of Student Affairs**: Student conduct and compliance

This distributed responsibility model ensures both academic and technical expertise inform policy implementation.

Progressive Implementation Strategy

Student Guidelines Framework

The policy recognizes AI as both a challenge and opportunity, establishing five core principles:

1. **Conditional Permission Model**: Students may use AI tools with explicit faculty authorization

2. **Academic Integrity Integration**: Clear connection to existing academic misconduct policies

3. **Original Work Requirements**: Emphasis on student ownership with appropriate citation

4. **Data Privacy Protection**: Mandatory awareness of third-party data sharing risks

5. **Equity Assurance**: Explicit commitment that no student will be disadvantaged by lack of AI access

Faculty and Staff Guidelines

The policy empowers faculty through:
- **Instructor Discretion**: Authority to set course-specific AI policies

- **Administrative Oversight**: Fact-checking requirements for AI-generated institutional content

- **Detection Tool Caution**: Recognition of AI detection limitations and false positives

Data Security and Privacy Framework

Risk Assessment Protocol
Before inputting "Restricted Data" into AI tools, TSU requires:
- Mandatory OTS security review
- Direct contact with technology services
- Approval process for sensitive information

Restricted Data Categories
The policy specifically protects:
- FERPA-protected educational records
- HIPAA-protected health information
- Personally identifiable information
- Employee performance records
- Proprietary intellectual property
- Confidential research data

Enforcement and Compliance Structure

Consequences Framework
- **Students**: Violations handled through Student Code of Conduct

- **Faculty & Staff**: Standard disciplinary processes apply

Oversight Mechanisms
- **Technical Monitoring**: OTS authority to block unauthorized AI tools

- **Regular Policy Reviews**: Alignment with legal and technological developments

- **Compliance Reporting**: Office of Risk and Financial Compliance oversight

Significance in Pioneering AI Policy Development

1. **Balanced Approach to Innovation and Integrity**
   TSU's policy demonstrates how institutions can embrace AI technology while maintaining academic standards. The policy states: "The University embraces the integration of AI with a commitment to scholarly rigor, intellectual integrity, and educational excellence."

2. Proactive Rather Than Reactive Framework
Unlike institutions that implement AI policies only after problems arise, TSU's comprehensive approach addresses potential issues before they become institutional challenges.

3. Stakeholder-Inclusive Development
The policy considers the needs of students, faculty, staff, and administrators, creating a unified institutional approach rather than siloed guidelines.

4. Legal and Regulatory Compliance
Explicit attention to Tennessee law, federal privacy regulations (FERPA, HIPAA), and intellectual property protections demonstrates sophisticated legal awareness.

5. Future-Oriented Design
The policy includes provisions for regular review and updates, acknowledging the rapidly evolving nature of AI technology.

Institutional Framework Development Model

Phase 1: Policy Foundation
- **Stakeholder Analysis**: Identify all university constituencies affected by AI integration

- **Regulatory Review**: Assess federal, state, and institutional legal requirements

- **Risk Assessment**: Evaluate data security, privacy, and academic integrity risks

Phase 2: Collaborative Development
- **Faculty Senate Involvement**: Ensure academic freedom and pedagogical autonomy

- **Student Input**: Address equity, accessibility, and learning support needs

- **Technical Infrastructure**: Coordinate with IT services for implementation capacity

Phase 3: Implementation Support
- **Professional Development**: Faculty training on AI integration and assessment modification

- **Student Education**: Digital literacy programs and AI ethics training

- **Resource Allocation**: Technology access and support systems

Phase 4: Continuous Improvement
- **Regular Assessment**: Monitor policy effectiveness and emerging challenges

- **Stakeholder Feedback**: Ongoing input from all university constituencies

- **Policy Updates**: Adapt to technological and regulatory changes

Key Success Factors

1. **Clear Authority Structure**: Designated responsible offices with specific roles

2. **Flexible Implementation**: Course-level discretion within institutional guidelines

3. **Security Integration**: Technical safeguards aligned with educational goals

4. **Equity Considerations**: Explicit attention to digital divide issues

5. **Professional Development**: Commitment to ongoing training and support

Conclusion

Tennessee State University's AI policy framework represents a pioneering approach to institutional AI integration that balances innovation with responsibility. By addressing technical, legal, educational, and ethical considerations within a unified policy framework, TSU provides a model for other institutions navigating the complex landscape of AI in higher education.

Academic Excellence Made Achievable: Your Gateway to Stress-Free Scholarly Success

Welcome to a revolutionary approach to academic writing that transforms the traditionally daunting journey of crafting papers, theses, and dissertations into an empowering and manageable experience. If you've ever felt overwhelmed by the prospect of producing high-caliber academic work while maintaining unwavering standards of integrity, you're about to discover that excellence and peace of mind can coexist beautifully.

Beyond the Myth of Academic Suffering

For too long, the academic community has perpetuated the myth that quality scholarship must come at the cost of sleepless nights, overwhelming stress, and constant anxiety. This manual shatters that misconception entirely. You're about to embark on a journey that proves rigorous academic work can be both deeply rewarding and surprisingly achievable when approached with the right tools and strategies.

The Power of Strategic Guidance

Within these pages lies something extraordinary: a comprehensive collection of meticulously crafted prompts designed to guide you through every conceivable stage of the academic writing process. These aren't generic suggestions or vague encouragements—they are precision-engineered tools that transform complex academic challenges into manageable, step-by-step processes.

Each prompt has been developed to address specific pain points that scholars encounter, from the initial spark of a research idea to the final polish of a completed manuscript. Whether you're grappling with literature reviews, methodology design, data analysis, or the art of academic argumentation, you'll find specialized prompts that illuminate the path forward with remarkable clarity.

Your Academic Integrity Companion

Every element of this manual has been designed with the highest standards of academic integrity at its core. These prompts don't shortcut the scholarly process—they enhance it, ensuring that your original thinking, critical analysis, and unique contributions shine through while providing the structural support you need to present your ideas with maximum impact and clarity.

What Awaits You

As you turn each page, you'll discover prompts that address the nuanced challenges of academic writing with surgical precision. You'll find guidance for crafting compelling research questions that captivate your readers, strategies for synthesizing complex literature that demonstrates your mastery of the field, and techniques for presenting your methodology with confidence and clarity.

But this is just the beginning. The real treasure lies in the advanced prompts that tackle the most sophisticated aspects of scholarly work—those that help you develop original theoretical frameworks, construct bulletproof arguments, and present findings that contribute meaningfully to your discipline.

Your Journey Starts Now

The academic excellence you've always envisioned is no longer a distant dream—it's an achievable reality waiting just beyond this introduction. The specialized prompts ahead will become your trusted companions, transforming what once seemed impossible into inevitable success.

Prepare to experience academic writing as it was meant to be: intellectually stimulating, professionally rewarding, and surprisingly stress-free. Your future self—the one holding that completed thesis or celebrating that published paper—is already thanking you for taking this first step.

The treasure trove of academic wisdom awaits. Turn the page and claim your path to scholarly excellence.

All the Best,

Robert O. Hassell, Ed.D., Author

Chapter 1
75 General AI Prompts for Topic Exploration, Research and Analysis

Chapter 1:
75 General AI Prompts for Topic Exploration, Research and Analysis

This foundational chapter provides versatile AI prompts designed to help researchers explore new topics, conduct preliminary research, and perform basic analysis across various academic disciplines. The prompts cover essential research activities such as identifying key themes, analyzing existing literature, developing research questions, and organizing complex information. These general-purpose prompts serve as starting points for academic inquiry and can be adapted to suit different fields of study, making them valuable tools for both novice and experienced researchers beginning their investigative journey.

How to Use These Prompts

For Students:
- Replace **[INSERT TOPIC]** with your specific area of interest
- Use multiple prompts to explore different dimensions of your topic
- Combine prompts for more complex analysis
- Adapt the complexity level to match your course requirements

For Educators:
- Select prompts appropriate to your course level and objectives
- Use as discussion starters, essay topics, or research assignments
- Modify prompts to include specific requirements or constraints
- Encourage students to build upon initial responses with follow-up analysis

Tips for Effective Use:
- Start with foundation prompts before moving to more complex analysis
- Use reliable, peer-reviewed sources for research
- Consider multiple perspectives and potential biases

- Document your sources and reasoning process
- Be prepared to refine your understanding as you gather more information

Research Foundation Prompts (15 prompts)

1. **Topic Mapping**: "Create a comprehensive overview of **[INSERT TOPIC]**. What are the key subtopics, major debates, and current trends in this field?"

2. **Multiple Perspectives**: "Analyze **[INSERT TOPIC]** from at least three different disciplinary perspectives. How does each field approach and understand this subject differently?"

3. **Historical Development**: "Trace the evolution of thinking about **[INSERT TOPIC]** over time. What major shifts in understanding have occurred and what caused them?"

4. **Current State Analysis**: "What is the current state of research/knowledge about **[INSERT TOPIC]**? What are the most recent developments and findings?"

5. **Controversy Exploration**: "Identify and analyze the main controversies or debates surrounding **[INSERT TOPIC]**. What evidence supports different sides?"

6. **Gap Identification**: "What gaps exist in current knowledge about **[INSERT TOPIC]**? What questions remain unanswered or under-researched?"

7. **Stakeholder Analysis**: "Who are the key stakeholders affected by **[INSERT TOPIC]**? How do their interests and perspectives differ?"

8. **Methodology Comparison**: "Compare different research methods used to study **[INSERT TOPIC]**. What are the strengths and limitations of each approach?"

9. **Cross-Cultural Examination**: "How is **[INSERT TOPIC]** understood or approached differently across various cultures or societies? What accounts for these differences?"

10. **Interdisciplinary Connections**: "How does **[INSERT TOPIC]** connect to or influence other fields of study? Map these interdisciplinary relationships."

11. **Evidence Evaluation**: "What types of evidence are most commonly used when studying

[INSERT TOPIC]? How reliable and valid is this evidence?"

12. **Theoretical Frameworks**: "What major theories or models are used to explain **[INSERT TOPIC]**? Compare their explanatory power and limitations."

13. **Scale Analysis**: "Examine **[INSERT TOPIC]** at different scales (individual, local, national, global). How does the perspective change at each level?"

14. **Future Implications**: "Based on current trends and research, what are the potential future developments related to **[INSERT TOPIC]**?"

15. **Source Diversity**: "Identify and analyze primary, secondary, and tertiary sources related to **[INSERT TOPIC]**. How do they complement each other?"

Critical Analysis Prompts (15 prompts)

1. **Assumption Challenge**: "What fundamental assumptions underlie common beliefs about [INSERT TOPIC]? Are these assumptions valid?"

2. **Bias Identification**: "What potential biases might influence how [INSERT TOPIC] is studied, reported, or understood? How can these be addressed?"

3. **Causation vs. Correlation**: "Examine claims about cause-and-effect relationships in [INSERT TOPIC]. Which are supported by evidence and which may be correlational?"

4. **Data Interpretation**: "Analyze conflicting data or statistics about [INSERT TOPIC]. What might account for these discrepancies?"

5. **Rhetorical Analysis**: "How is [INSERT TOPIC] presented in different media sources? What rhetorical strategies are used to influence public opinion?"

6. **Logical Fallacies**: "Identify common logical fallacies in arguments about [INSERT TOPIC]. How do these weaken the quality of debate?"

7. **Context Importance**: "How does context (historical, cultural, economic, etc.) shape understanding of **[INSERT TOPIC]**? Provide specific examples."

8. **Counterargument Exploration**: "What are the strongest counterarguments to popular positions on **[INSERT TOPIC]**? How compelling are they?"

9. **Definition Disputes**: "How is **[INSERT TOPIC]** defined differently by various experts or groups? Why do these definitional differences matter?"

10. **Unintended Consequences**: "What unintended consequences have resulted from policies, interventions, or developments related to **[INSERT TOPIC]**?"

11. **Power Dynamics**: "Who has the power to shape narratives about **[INSERT TOPIC]**? How does this influence public understanding?"

12. **Ethical Dimensions**: "What ethical considerations surround **[INSERT TOPIC]**? How do different ethical frameworks approach these issues?"

13. **Generalization Limits**: "What are the limits of generalizing findings about **[INSERT TOPIC]** across different populations or contexts?"

14. **Quality Standards**: "What criteria should be used to evaluate the quality of research or information about **[INSERT TOPIC]**?"

15. **Perspective Blind Spots**: "What perspectives or voices are typically missing from discussions about **[INSERT TOPIC]**? Why might this occur?"

Comparative Analysis Prompts (15 prompts)

1. **Case Study Comparison**: "Compare how **[INSERT TOPIC]** manifests in 3-5 different real-world cases. What patterns and differences emerge?"

2. **Model Comparison**: "Compare different theoretical models or approaches to **[INSERT TOPIC]**. What are their relative strengths and weaknesses?"

3. **Solution Comparison**: "Analyze different proposed solutions to problems related to

[INSERT TOPIC]. What evidence supports their effectiveness?"

4. **System Comparison**: "How do different systems (political, economic, educational, etc.) address [INSERT TOPIC]? What can we learn from these variations?"

5. **Temporal Comparison**: "Compare how [INSERT TOPIC] was understood and addressed in different historical periods. What has changed and what has remained constant?"

6. **Geographic Comparison**: "How does [INSERT TOPIC] vary across different geographic regions? What factors account for these variations?"

7. **Demographic Comparison**: "How does [INSERT TOPIC] affect or relate to different demographic groups? What accounts for these differences?"

8. **Institutional Comparison**: "Compare how different institutions (universities, governments, organizations) approach [INSERT TOPIC]. What best practices emerge?"

9. **Media Comparison**: "How is [INSERT TOPIC] portrayed across different media

platforms or outlets? What biases or emphases are evident?"

10. **Policy Comparison**: "Compare different policy approaches to **[INSERT TOPIC]** across jurisdictions. What outcomes have resulted?"

11. **Expert vs. Public Opinion**: "How do expert opinions on **[INSERT TOPIC]** differ from public perceptions? What might account for these gaps?"

12. **Quantitative vs. Qualitative**: "Compare quantitative and qualitative research findings about **[INSERT TOPIC]**. Do they tell consistent stories?"

13. **Cost-Benefit Analysis**: "Compare the costs and benefits of different approaches to **[INSERT TOPIC]**. How should trade-offs be evaluated?"

14. **Short-term vs. Long-term**: "How do short-term and long-term perspectives on **[INSERT TOPIC]** differ? Which should be prioritized?"

15. **Industry Comparison**: "How do different industries or sectors approach **[INSERT TOPIC]**? What factors drive these differences?"

Synthesis and Innovation Prompts (15 prompts)

1. **Pattern Recognition**: "What patterns can you identify across different aspects or examples of **[INSERT TOPIC]**? What do these patterns suggest?"

2. **Knowledge Integration**: "Integrate insights from multiple disciplines to create a more comprehensive understanding of **[INSERT TOPIC]**."

3. **Novel Connections**: "What unexpected or underexplored connections exist between **[INSERT TOPIC]** and other areas of study?"

4. **Scenario Building**: "Develop 3-5 plausible future scenarios related to **[INSERT TOPIC]**. What factors would influence which scenario unfolds?"

5. **Framework Development**: "Based on your research, develop a new framework for understanding or analyzing **[INSERT TOPIC]**."

6. **Best Practice Synthesis**: "Synthesize research to identify best practices related to

[INSERT TOPIC]. What evidence supports these recommendations?"

7. **Meta-Analysis**: "Conduct a meta-analysis of research findings about **[INSERT TOPIC]**. What overarching conclusions can be drawn?"

8. **Innovation Opportunities**: "Based on current limitations or gaps, what innovations could advance understanding or practice related to **[INSERT TOPIC]**?"

9. **Principle Extraction**: "What fundamental principles or laws govern **[INSERT TOPIC]**? How universally applicable are these principles?"

10. **System Mapping**: "Create a comprehensive system map showing how different elements related to **[INSERT TOPIC]** interact and influence each other."

11. **Paradox Resolution**: "Identify and propose resolutions to paradoxes or contradictions within **[INSERT TOPIC]**."

12. **Narrative Synthesis**: "Synthesize diverse perspectives on **[INSERT TOPIC]** into a coherent narrative that acknowledges complexity and nuance."

13. **Predictive Modeling**: "Based on available data and trends, develop a model to predict future developments in **[INSERT TOPIC]**."

14. **Design Thinking**: "Apply design thinking principles to reimagine approaches to challenges related to **[INSERT TOPIC]**."

15. **Wisdom Distillation**: "Distill the most important insights about **[INSERT TOPIC]** into key principles or guidelines for practitioners."

Application and Evaluation Prompts (15 prompts)

1. **Real-World Application**: "How can theoretical knowledge about **[INSERT TOPIC]** be applied to solve real-world problems? Provide specific examples."

2. **Implementation Challenges**: "What obstacles typically arise when implementing solutions related to **[INSERT TOPIC]**? How can these be overcome?"

3. **Success Metrics**: "How should success be measured when addressing issues related to **[INSERT TOPIC]**? What indicators are most meaningful?"

4. **Scalability Analysis**: "Analyze the scalability of different approaches to **[INSERT TOPIC]**. What works at small scale vs. large scale?"

5. **Resource Requirements**: "What resources (time, money, expertise, technology) are needed to effectively address **[INSERT TOPIC]**?"

6. **Risk Assessment**: "What risks are associated with different approaches to **[INSERT TOPIC]**? How can these risks be mitigated?"

7. **Feasibility Study**: "Assess the feasibility of implementing a specific solution related to **[INSERT TOPIC]** in a particular context."
8. **Impact Evaluation**: "How can the impact of interventions related to **[INSERT TOPIC]** be accurately measured and evaluated?"

9. **Adaptation Strategies**: "How can approaches to **[INSERT TOPIC]** be adapted for different contexts, cultures, or populations?"

10. **Sustainability Assessment**: "Evaluate the long-term sustainability of different approaches to

[INSERT TOPIC]. What factors affect sustainability?"

11. **Technology Integration**: "How can technology be leveraged to better understand or address **[INSERT TOPIC]** What are the limitations?"

12. **Policy Recommendations**: "Based on your analysis of **[INSERT TOPIC]**, what policy recommendations would you make? What evidence supports these?"

13. **Communication Strategy**: "How can complex information about **[INSERT TOPIC]** be effectively communicated to different audiences?"

14. **Monitoring and Evaluation**: "Design a system for monitoring progress and evaluating outcomes related to **[INSERT TOPIC]**." **Continuous Improvement**:

15. How can approaches to **[INSERT TOPIC]** be continuously improved based on feedback and new evidence? What learning mechanisms are needed?"

Chapter 2
75 Dissertation Research AI Prompts for Literature Reviews, Methodologies, Introductions, and Future Research

Chapter 2: 75 Dissertation Research AI Prompts for Literature Reviews, Methodologies, Introductions, and Future Research

This chapter focuses on the core components of dissertation writing, offering specialized prompts to guide researchers through critical sections of their academic work. The prompts address literature review synthesis, methodology selection and justification, compelling introduction crafting, and identifying future research directions. These targeted prompts help doctoral students navigate the complex process of academic writing by providing structured approaches to developing comprehensive literature reviews, defending methodological choices, establishing research context, and contributing to scholarly discourse.

How to Use These Dissertation Prompts For Doctoral Students:

Literature Review Phase:
• Use prompts 1-20 to conduct comprehensive literature analysis.
• Start with broad mapping prompts, then focus on specific gaps and contradictions.
• Combine multiple prompts to create multifaceted literature reviews.

Methodology Development:
• Use prompts 21-40 to design rigorous research approaches.
• Match methodology prompts to your research philosophy and questions.
• Consider innovative combinations of traditional and emerging methods.

Introduction and Problem Formulation:
• Use prompts 41-55 to craft compelling research introductions.
• Ensure logical flow from problem identification to research contribution.
• Use these prompts iteratively to refine your research focus.

Future Research Planning:
•	Use prompts 56-75 to identify future directions.
•	These can inform your conclusion chapters and post-doctoral research plans.
•	Consider which ideas could form collaborative research programs.

For Dissertation Supervisors:
•	Use prompts as discussion starters in supervision meetings.
•	Assign specific prompts to help students think through methodological challenges.
•	Encourage students to work through multiple prompts to develop comprehensive understanding.

Best Practices:
•	Replace [INSERT TOPIC] and [research question] with your specific focus area.
•	Use multiple prompts in combination for comprehensive analysis.
•	Document insights and decisions from each prompt exploration.
•	Return to prompts periodically as your research evolves.
•	Adapt prompt complexity to match your stage in the doctoral process.

Literature Review Prompts (20 prompts)

1. **Systematic Literature Mapping:** "Conduct a systematic review of the last 15 years of research on **[INSERT TOPIC]**. What theoretical frameworks dominate, and how has the conceptual landscape evolved?"

2. **Theoretical Gap Analysis:** "Identify theoretical gaps in the current literature on **[INSERT TOPIC]**. Where do existing theories fail to explain observed phenomena or contradictory findings?"

3. **Methodological Synthesis:** "Analyze the methodological approaches used in **[INSERT TOPIC]** research over the past decade. What methodological blind spots or limitations consistently appear?"

4. **Cross-Disciplinary Integration:** "How has **[INSERT TOPIC]** been approached differently across disciplines? Where do disciplinary boundaries create artificial separations in understanding?"

5. **Seminal Work Influence:** "Trace the intellectual genealogy of **[INSERT TOPIC]** by

identifying seminal works and analyzing how they've influenced subsequent research trajectories."

6. **Paradigm Shift Analysis:** "Identify paradigm shifts in **[INSERT TOPIC]** research. What triggered these shifts, and how have they redefined research questions and methods?"

7. **Geographic and Cultural Bias:** "Examine the geographic and cultural distribution of **[INSERT TOPIC]** research. What populations, contexts, or perspectives are over- or under-represented?"

8. **Temporal Research Patterns:** "Analyze how research focus on **[INSERT TOPIC]** has shifted over time. What external factors (technological, social, political) have influenced these changes?"

9. **Citation Network Analysis:** "Map the citation networks in **[INSERT TOPIC]** research. Which works are most influential, and what does this reveal about knowledge production in the field?"

10. **Findings Synthesis:** "Systematically analyze contradictory findings in **[INSERT TOPIC]** research. What methodological,

contextual, or theoretical factors might explain these discrepancies?"

11. **Emerging Subfield Identification:** "Identify emerging subfields or research directions within **[INSERT TOPIC]**. What new questions are researchers beginning to explore?"

12. **Meta-Theoretical Analysis:** "Examine the meta-theoretical assumptions underlying **[INSERT TOPIC]** research. How do different ontological and epistemological positions shape research approaches?"

13. **Research Quality Assessment:** "Develop criteria for assessing the quality and rigor of **[INSERT TOPIC]** research. How do current studies measure against these standards?"

14. **Conceptual Boundary Definition:** "How is **[INSERT TOPIC]** defined and bounded differently across studies? What are the implications of these definitional variations?"

15. **Longitudinal Trend Analysis:** "Analyze long-term trends in **[INSERT TOPIC]** research. What cyclical patterns or persistent themes emerge over extended periods?"

16. **Interdisciplinary Synthesis Opportunities:** "Identify opportunities for interdisciplinary synthesis in **[INSERT TOPIC]** research. Where could cross-pollination enhance understanding?"

17. **Power Structure Analysis:** "Examine the power structures within **[INSERT TOPIC]** research communities. Who are the gatekeepers, and how do they influence research directions?"

18. **Theoretical Saturation Assessment:** "Assess areas of theoretical saturation versus innovation in **[INSERT TOPIC]** research. Where is the field recycling ideas versus generating new insights?"

19. **Infrastructure Analysis:** "Analyze the research infrastructure supporting **[INSERT TOPIC]** studies. What funding patterns, institutional support, and collaborative networks exist?"

20. **Translation and Application Gaps:** "Identify gaps between **[INSERT TOPIC]** research findings and their translation into practice, policy, or real-world applications."

Methodology Design Prompts (20 prompts)

1. **Research Philosophy Alignment:** "Justify your choice of research philosophy (positivist, interpretivist, pragmatist, etc.) for investigating **[Research Question]**. How does this philosophy shape your methodological choices?"

2. **Mixed Methods Integration:** "Design a mixed-methods approach for **[research question]**. How will quantitative and qualitative components be integrated for maximum synergy?"

3. **Sampling Strategy Optimization:** "Develop a sophisticated sampling strategy for **[Population/Context]**. How will you balance representativeness, accessibility, and theoretical relevance?"

4. **Validity and Reliability Framework:** "Construct a comprehensive validity and reliability framework for your **[INSERT TOPIC]** study. How will you address internal, external, construct, and statistical conclusion validity?"

5. **Ethical Considerations Deep Dive:** "Conduct a thorough ethical analysis of your proposed **[INSERT TOPIC]** research. What potential harm, consent, confidentiality, and power imbalance issues must be addressed?"

6. **Collection Innovation:** "Design innovative data collection methods for **[Research Context]**. How can traditional approaches be enhanced or new methods developed?"

7. **Triangulation Strategy:** "Develop a triangulation strategy using multiple data sources, methods, investigators, or theories for **[Research Question]**. How will convergence and divergence be interpreted?"

8. **Longitudinal Design Considerations:** "Design a longitudinal study for **[Phenomenon]**. What are the trade-offs between different temporal designs, and how will you address attrition and maturation effects?"

9. **Cross-Cultural Methodology:** "Adapt your methodology for cross-cultural **[INSERT TOPIC]** research. What cultural considerations affect data collection, interpretation, and validity?"

10. **Digital Methods Integration:** "Integrate digital research methods (social media analysis, web scraping, digital ethnography) into your **[INSERT TOPIC]** study. What are the methodological implications?"

11. **Participatory Research Design:** "Design a participatory or community-based approach to **[INSERT TOPIC]** research. How will you balance academic rigor with community ownership and benefit?"

12. **Case Study Framework:** "Develop a comparative case study methodology for **[Phenomenon]**. How will case selection, data collection, and cross-case analysis be structured?"

13. **Intervention Study Design:** "Design a rigorous intervention study for **[INSERT TOPIC]**. How will you establish causality while addressing real-world complexity?"

14. **Grounded Theory Application:** "Apply grounded theory methodology to **[Research Question]**. How will theoretical sampling, constant comparison, and theoretical saturation be achieved?"

15. **Phenomenological Method Design:** "Design a phenomenological study of **[Lived Experience]**. How will you achieve epoché, phenomenological reduction, and imaginative variation?"

16. **Action Research Framework:** "Develop an action research approach to **[Practical Problem]**. How will you balance research rigor with practical problem-solving and stakeholder engagement?"

17. **Discourse Analysis Methodology:** "Design a discourse analysis study of **[INSERT TOPIC]**. What theoretical framework will guide your analysis, and how will you ensure analytical rigor?"

18. **Big Data Analytics Integration:** "Integrate big data analytics into traditional **[INSERT TOPIC]** research methods. What are the epistemological and methodological implications?"

19. Experimental Design Optimization: "Optimize an experimental design for **[Hypothesis]**. How will you control confounding variables while maintaining ecological validity?"

20. **Methodological Reflexivity Framework:** "Develop a framework for methodological

reflexivity in **[INSERT TOPIC]** research. How will you acknowledge, and address researcher influence throughout the study?"

Introduction and Problem Formulation Prompts (15 prompts)

1. **Problem Statement Precision:** "Craft a precise problem statement for **[INSERT TOPIC]** that clearly articulates the gap between current knowledge and what needs to be known. Why does this gap matter?"

2. **Research Question Hierarchy:** "Develop a hierarchy of research questions for **[INSERT TOPIC]**, including primary questions, sub-questions, and hypotheses. How do they logically connect?"

3. **Significance Justification:** "Justify the significance of your **[INSERT TOPIC]** research from theoretical, methodological, practical, and social perspectives. Who benefits and how?"

4. **Conceptual Framework Development:** "Develop a conceptual framework that maps the key concepts, variables, and relationships in your

[INSERT TOPIC] study. How does this framework guide your research?"

5. **Assumption Articulation:** "Explicitly articulate the assumptions underlying your [INSERT TOPIC] research. How might these assumptions limit or bias your findings?"

6. **Boundary Setting:** "Clearly define the boundaries of your [INSERT TOPIC] study. What will be included, excluded, and why? How do these boundaries affect generalizability?"

7. **Context Positioning:** "Position your [INSERT TOPIC] research within its historical, cultural, social, and institutional context. How does context shape the research problem?"

8. **Stakeholder Analysis:** "Identify and analyze all stakeholders affected by your [INSERT TOPIC] research. How will different groups use or be impacted by your findings?"

9. **Research Contribution Articulation:** "Articulate the specific contributions your [INSERT TOPIC] research will make to knowledge, theory, method, and practice. What will be new or different?"

10. **Definitional Precision:** "Provide precise operational definitions for all key concepts in your **[INSERT TOPIC]** study. How do these definitions relate to existing literature?"

11. **Research Rationale Construction:** "Construct a compelling rationale for why your **[INSERT TOPIC]** research is needed now. What convergence of factors makes this study timely and important?"

12. **Theoretical Foundation Establishment:** "Establish the theoretical foundation for your **[INSERT TOPIC]** research. Which theories inform your study, and how do they interconnect?"

13. **Methodological Positioning:** "Position your methodological approach within the broader methodological landscape of **[INSERT TOPIC]** research. Why is your approach appropriate and innovative?"

14. **Research Scope Optimization:** "Optimize the scope of your **[INSERT TOPIC]** research to balance ambition with feasibility. What trade-offs are necessary, and how do you justify them?"

15. **Problem Complexity Acknowledgment:** "Acknowledge and address the complexity of your **[INSERT TOPIC]** research problem. How will you manage complexity while maintaining analytical clarity?"

Future Research and Innovation Prompts (20 prompts)

1. **Research Agenda Development:** "Based on your **[INSERT TOPIC]** research, develop a 10-year research agenda for the field. What are the most promising directions for future investigation?"

2. **Methodological Innovation Opportunities:** "Identify opportunities for methodological innovation in **[INSERT TOPIC]** research. What new methods, technologies, or approaches could advance the field?"

3. **Interdisciplinary Collaboration Potential:** "Map potential interdisciplinary collaborations that could advance **[INSERT TOPIC]** research. What would each discipline contribute to these partnerships?"

4. **Technology Integration Roadmap:** "Develop a roadmap for integrating emerging technologies (AI, VR, blockchain, IoT, etc.) into **[INSERT TOPIC]** research. What are the possibilities and challenges?"

5. **Longitudinal Research Framework:** "Design a multi-decade longitudinal research framework for **[INSERT TOPIC]**. What would such a study reveal that shorter studies cannot?"

6. **Global Research Coordination:** "Propose a framework for coordinating **[INSERT TOPIC]** research globally. How could international collaboration address current limitations?"

7. **Theoretical Innovation Directions:** "Identify directions for theoretical innovation in **[INSERT TOPIC]**. Where are new theories needed, and what might they look like?"

8. **Policy Research Interface:** "Develop recommendations for strengthening the interface between **[INSERT TOPIC]** research and policy development. What mechanisms would improve evidence-based policy?"

9. **Replication and Validation Priorities:** "Identify the most important **[INSERT TOPIC]** findings that require replication or validation. What systematic replication program would strengthen the field?"

10. **Research Translation Enhancement:** "Propose strategies for enhancing the translation of **[INSERT TOPIC]** research into practice. What barriers exist, and how can they be overcome?"

11. **Emerging Population Studies:** "Identify emerging populations or contexts that should be prioritized in future **[INSERT TOPIC]** research. What unique insights might these groups provide?"

12. **Causal Mechanism Exploration:** "Outline future research needed to understand causal mechanisms in **[INSERT TOPIC]**. What studies would provide the strongest causal evidence?"

13. **Scale and Scope Expansion:** "Propose how **[INSERT TOPIC]** research could be expanded in scale and scope. What would mega-studies or meta-analyses contribute?"

14. **Ethical Framework Evolution:** "Anticipate how considerations in **[INSERT TOPIC]** research

might evolve. What new ethical challenges will emerge, and how should the field prepare?"

15. **Research Infrastructure Development:** "Propose infrastructure development priorities for **[INSERT TOPIC]** research. What data repositories, research networks, or technological platforms are needed?"

16. **Training and Capacity Building:** "Develop recommendations for training the next generation of **[INSERT TOPIC]** researchers. What skills, knowledge, and perspectives will they need?"

17. **Public Engagement Innovation:** "Design innovative approaches for engaging the public with **[INSERT TOPIC]** research. How can researchers better communicate with and involve communities?"

18. **Research Impact Measurement:** "Propose new frameworks for measuring the impact of **[INSERT TOPIC]** research beyond traditional academic metrics. What indicators would better capture societal benefit?"

19. **Sustainability Research Integration:** "Explore how sustainability considerations could be better integrated into **[INSERT TOPIC]**

research. What would environmentally and socially sustainable research look like?"

20. **Research Democratization:** "Propose strategies for democratizing **[INSERT TOPIC]** research. How could community members, practitioners, and other stakeholders become more involved in research processes?"

Chapter 3
75 Dissertation Research AI Prompts Based on AQR Academic Quality Review Checklist

Chapter 3: 75 Dissertation Research AI Prompts Based on AQR Academic Quality Review Checklist

Drawing from established academic quality standards, this chapter presents prompts specifically aligned with Academic Quality Review (AQR) criteria and best practices. These prompts ensure that dissertation research meets rigorous academic standards by addressing elements such as theoretical framework development, research design validity, data analysis rigor, and scholarly contribution assessment. The chapter serves as a quality assurance tool, helping researchers evaluate and improve their work against established academic benchmarks while maintaining scholarly integrity throughout the research process.

Chapter 1: Introduction to the Study (15 prompts)

Abstract and Introduction Development

1. **Abstract Precision**: "Create a comprehensive abstract for **[INSERT TOPIC]** that includes: purpose of study, theoretical foundation, research questions in narrative format, sample, location, methodology, design, data analysis approach, and anticipated results. Ensure it follows APA format requirements."

2. **Research Focus Introduction**: "Develop an engaging introduction for **[INSERT TOPIC]** that introduces the dissertation topic, explains why this study is worth conducting, and provides an overview of chapter contents. How will you capture reader interest while maintaining academic rigor?"

3. **Study Value Articulation**: "Articulate the value and importance of conducting research on **[INSERT TOPIC]**. What makes this study timely, relevant, and necessary for the field? How does it address current needs or gaps?"

Background and Problem Development

4. **Historical Context Mapping**: "Trace the historical evolution of **[problem/topic]** from its origins to its current state. How has the problem developed over time, and what factors have contributed to its current form?"

5. **Literature Gap Identification**: "Based on current literature on **[INSERT TOPIC]**, identify the specific 'gap' or 'need' that exists. How does this gap lead to your problem statement and research focus?"

6. **Problem Statement Precision**: "Craft a precise problem statement for **[INSERT TOPIC]** that begins with 'It is not known if and to what degree/extent...' (quantitative) or 'It is not known how or why...' (qualitative). Identify the affected population and explain how your study will contribute to solving this problem."

Purpose and Research Questions

7. **Purpose Statement Development**: "Create a declarative purpose statement: 'The purpose of this study is...' **[that identifies your research methodology and design, target population, geographic location,**

and variables (quantitative) or phenomena (qualitative) to be studied."]

8. **Research Questions Alignment**: "Develop research questions that directly address your problem statement. **[For quantitative studies, include corresponding hypotheses. How do these questions narrow the focus while maintaining alignment with your purpose?"]**

9. **Methodology Justification**: "Justify why **[qualitative/quantitative/mixed methods]** methodology is the best approach for your **[INSERT TOPIC]** study. Compare it to alternative methodologies and explain why your choice is optimal for answering your research questions."

Significance and Theoretical Foundation

10. **Knowledge Advancement**: "Describe how your **[INSERT TOPIC]** research will advance scientific knowledge. What specific 'gap' or 'need' will it address, and how will it contribute to the existing body of literature?"

11. **Theoretical Foundation Connection**: "Identify the theory(ies) or model(s) that provide the foundation for your **[INSERT

TOPIC] study. How does your research connect to and extend these theoretical frameworks?"

12. **Significance Articulation**: "Describe the significance of your **[INSERT TOPIC]** study from three perspectives: academic research contribution, practical contribution to the field, and value to the population/community/society."

Research Design and Definitions

13. **Research Design Rationale**: "Describe your specific research design for **[INSERT TOPIC]** and justify why it's the best approach compared to alternative designs. How will this design facilitate data collection to answer your research questions?"

14. **Operational Definitions**: "Develop precise operational definitions for all key concepts, variables (quantitative), or phenomena (qualitative) in your **[INSERT TOPIC]** study. Support each definition with scholarly citations."

15. **Assumptions and Limitations**: "Identify and justify the methodological, theoretical,

and topic-specific assumptions for your **[INSERT TOPIC]** study. What limitations and delimitations must be acknowledged, and how might they affect your findings?"

Chapter 2: Literature Review (20 prompts)

Literature Review Structure and Organization

1. **Literature Review Framework**: "Design a comprehensive organizational framework for your **[INSERT TOPIC]** literature review. What major themes, sections, and subsections will provide logical structure for your minimum 30-page review?"

2. **Search Strategy Documentation**: "Document your literature search strategy for **[INSERT TOPIC]**. What databases, search terms, inclusion/exclusion criteria, and time parameters did you use? How does this demonstrate thoroughness?"

3. **Historical Problem Evolution**: "Analyze how the **[Problem/Topic]** has evolved historically through the literature. What key developments, paradigm shifts, or theoretical advances have shaped current understanding?"

Theoretical Foundations and Conceptual Framework

4. **Theoretical Framework Deep Dive**: "Conduct an in-depth analysis of the theory(ies) or model(s) that provide your study's foundation. How do seminal sources define these frameworks, and how do they apply to your **[INSERT TOPIC]** research?"

5. **Conceptual Framework Development**: "Build a logical argument connecting your theoretical foundation to your research questions. How does the theoretical framework directly inform and support your specific research approach?"

6. **Theory-Research Alignment**: "Demonstrate how your research questions align with your theoretical foundation. What aspects of the theory will your study test, extend, or apply to **[specific context]**?"

Variable and Phenomena Analysis

7. **Variable Literature Synthesis**: "For quantitative studies: Synthesize literature on each research variable in your **[INSERT TOPIC]** study. What prior empirical

research exists on these variables and their relationships?"

8. **Phenomena Exploration**: "For qualitative studies: Synthesize literature exploring the phenomena central to your **[INSERT TOPIC]** study. How have previous researchers investigated and understood these phenomena?"

9. **Relationship Mapping**: "Map the relationships between key concepts/variables in your **[INSERT TOPIC]** literature. What connections, contradictions, or gaps emerge from existing research?"

Thematic Literature Organization

10. **Theme Development**: "Organize your **[INSERT TOPIC]** literature into coherent themes or topics. For each theme, provide an introductory paragraph explaining its relevance to your study and a summary paragraph comparing/contrasting perspective."

11. **Empirical Research Synthesis**: "Synthesize empirical research findings related to **[INSERT TOPIC]**. Include actual data and results, not just summaries.

How do findings converge or diverge across studies?"

12. **Comparative Perspective Analysis**: "Compare and contrast alternative perspectives on **[INSERT TOPIC]** within the literature. What different schools of thought, approaches, or findings exist, and how do you reconcile contradictions?"

Methodological Literature Review

13. **Methodology Literature Analysis**: "Analyze and synthesize methodological approaches used in **[INSERT TOPIC]** research. What designs, data collection methods, and analytical techniques have been employed? What are their strengths and limitations?"

14. **Instrumentation Justification**: "Review literature on instruments and measures used in **[INSERT TOPIC]** research. Based on this review, justify your choice of data collection instruments or measurement approaches."

15. **Sampling Strategy Literature**: "Examine how other researchers have approached sampling in **[INSERT TOPIC]** studies. What can you learn about effective

sampling strategies for your population and research questions?"

Source Quality and Integration

16. **Source Quality Assessment**: "Evaluate the quality and credibility of sources in your **[INSERT TOPIC]** literature review. How do you balance seminal works, recent empirical studies, and authoritative sources?"

17. **Citation Network Analysis**: "Analyze citation patterns in **[INSERT TOPIC]** literature. Which works are most frequently cited, and what does this reveal about knowledge building in your field?"

18. **Research Gap Articulation**: "Based on your comprehensive literature review, clearly articulate the specific gaps that justify your **[INSERT TOPIC]** study. How do these gaps connect to your problem statement and research questions?"

Literature Synthesis and Summary

19. **Cross-Study Synthesis**: "Synthesize findings across multiple studies in your **[INSERT TOPIC]** review. What patterns, trends, or consistent findings emerge?

Where do inconsistencies require further investigation?"

20. **Literature Summary Integration**: "Create a comprehensive summary that integrates all sections of your literature review. How do the theoretical foundations, empirical research, and methodological considerations converge to support your study design?"

Chapter 3: Methodology (20 prompts)

Research Philosophy and Design

1. **Methodology Elaboration**: "Elaborate on your chosen research methodology for **[INSERT TOPIC]**. Provide detailed rationale supported by empirical literature for why this methodology is superior to alternatives for addressing your research questions."

2. **Research Design Justification**: "Justify your specific research design using authoritative sources. How does this design optimally collect the data needed to answer your research questions compared to alternative designs?"

3. **Paradigm Alignment**: "Demonstrate how your research philosophy (positivist, interpretivist, pragmatist) aligns with your methodology and design choices for **[INSERT TOPIC]**. What epistemological assumptions guide your approach?"

Population and Sampling

4. **Population Definition Framework**: "Define your general population, target population, and study sample for **[INSERT TOPIC]**. How do geographic, demographic, and inclusion criteria create a well-defined sampling frame?"

5. **Sample Size Justification**: "Justify your sample size based on your research design and empirical literature. **[For quantitative studies, meet minimum requirements (50 cases or 40 per cell). For qualitative studies, justify adequacy for data saturation."]**

6. **Sampling Strategy Design**: "Design and justify your sampling procedures **(convenience, purposive, random, etc.)** using scholarly sources. How will you recruit, select, and assign participants while minimizing bias?"

Data Collection Instruments and Procedures

7. **Instrumentation Selection**: "Provide detailed justification for your data collection instruments. Include reliability and validity statistics, structure descriptions, and citations from original sources or validation studies."
8. **Data Collection Protocol**: "Develop a detailed data collection protocol that another researcher could replicate. Include step-by-step procedures, timing, participant interactions, and quality control measures."

9. **Reliability and Validity Framework**: "Establish the reliability and validity of your data collection approach. For quantitative studies, provide specific statistics. For qualitative studies, describe trustworthiness strategies."

Data Analysis Planning

10. **Analysis Strategy Alignment**: "Describe in detail your data analysis procedures, organized by research question. How do your analytical techniques align with your research design and question types?"

11. **Statistical Analysis Justification**: "For quantitative studies: Justify your choice of

statistical tests, significance levels, and assumption testing procedures. How do these align with your data types and research questions?"

12. **Qualitative Analysis Framework**: "For qualitative studies: Detail your coding procedures, theme development process, and validity strategies. How will you ensure rigor and credibility in your analysis?"

Data Management and Ethics

13. **Data Management Protocol**: "Develop comprehensive data management procedures for both collection and storage. Address security, confidentiality, retention periods, and disposal methods."

14. **Ethical Considerations Framework**: "Conduct a thorough ethical analysis of your [INSERT TOPIC] study. Address informed consent, potential risks/benefits, anonymity/confidentiality, and protection of vulnerable populations."

15. **IRB Preparation**: "Prepare materials for IRB review including informed consent documents, recruitment materials, and risk assessment. How do you minimize potential harm while maximizing research benefits?"

Limitations and Quality Assurance

16. **Limitation Identification**: "Identify and discuss limitations related to your methodology, sample, instrumentation, and data collection. Why are these limitations unavoidable, and how will you minimize their impact?"

17. **Delimitation Justification**: "Clearly define your study's boundaries and delimitations. What conscious choices limit your study's scope, and how do these choices serve your research purposes?"

18. **Quality Control Measures**: "Describe quality control measures throughout your research process. How will you ensure data quality, reduce bias, and maintain consistency in data collection and analysis?"

Research Alignment and Integration

19. **Ten Strategic Points Alignment**: "Demonstrate alignment among your problem statement, research questions, methodology, design, instrumentation, data collection, and analysis procedures. How do all elements work together coherently?"

20. **Methodological Coherence**: "Show how your methodology chapter integrates with and expands upon Chapters 1 and 2. How does your approach logically flow from your literature review and theoretical foundation?"

Chapter 4: Data Analysis and Results (10 prompts)

Results Presentation and Organization

1. **Results Organization Framework**: "Organize your **[INSERT TOPIC]** results presentation by research question or hypothesis. How will you present findings in a clear, non-evaluative manner that directly addresses each research question?"

2. **Descriptive Data Presentation**: "Present comprehensive descriptive data about your sample/population characteristics. Include narrative summaries and appropriate visual organizers (tables, charts, graphs) to enhance readability."

3. **Statistical Results Reporting**: "For quantitative studies: Report statistical results in proper format including test statistics, p-values, effect sizes, and

confidence intervals. Include tests of assumptions and power analysis as appropriate."

4. **Qualitative Findings Presentation**: "For qualitative studies: Present themes, patterns, and findings with supporting quotes and examples. How do you balance rich description with analytical rigor?"

Data Analysis Procedures Documentation

5. **Analysis Process Documentation**: "Document your actual data analysis procedures, including any deviations from your planned approach. If procedures differ from Chapter 3, explain and justify the changes."

6. **Data Quality Assessment**: "Assess and report data quality issues including missing data, outliers, assumption violations, or other limitations. How do these affect the interpretation of your results?"

Visual Data Presentation

7. **Graphic Organizer Optimization**: "Create effective tables, charts, graphs, and figures to display your data. How do these

visual elements enhance understanding and support your narrative results?"

8. **Results Summary Integration**: "Provide a concise summary that separates factual findings from interpretation. How do your results directly answer each research question while preparing readers for Chapter 5 discussion?"

Results Validation and Reliability

9. **Findings Validation**: "Demonstrate that your results are supported by sufficient quantity and quality of data. How do you establish credibility and trustworthiness of your findings?"

10. **Limitation Acknowledgment**: "Discuss any limitations that emerged during data analysis and how they affect interpretation. What new limitations became apparent through your analytical process?"

Chapter 5: Summary, Conclusions, and Recommendations (10 prompts)

Study Integration and Conclusions

1. **Comprehensive Study Summary**: "Provide a comprehensive summary of your entire **[INSERT TOPIC]** study that integrates findings with your original purpose, research questions, and theoretical framework. How does everything connect?"

2. **Findings Synthesis**: "Synthesize your study findings in the context of prior research from Chapter 2. How do your results compare, contrast, and advance the existing body of knowledge?"

3. **Theoretical Implications Analysis**: "Examine your findings in light of your theoretical framework. How do your results support, challenge, or extend the theories that guided your study?"

Implications Development

4. **Practical Implications Framework**: "Develop practical implications based on your findings. Who will benefit from implementing your results, and what specific

actions can practitioners take in work or educational settings?"

5. **Future Research Agenda**: "Propose 4-6 specific recommendations for future research based on your findings. What gaps remain, what new questions emerged, and how should the field advance?"

Recommendations and Impact

6. **Practice Recommendations**: "Generate 2-5 evidence-based recommendations for future practice. How can your findings be translated into actionable guidelines for practitioners?"

7. **Study Significance Reflection**: "Reflect on how your study achieved its intended significance as outlined in Chapter 1. What contributions did you actually make to knowledge, theory, and practice?"

8. **Methodological Contributions**: "Assess the methodological contributions of your study. What did you learn about research approaches in [INSERT TOPIC] that could inform future studies?"

Research Impact and Dissemination

9. **Knowledge Dissemination Strategy**: "Develop a strategy for disseminating your research findings. What audiences need this information, and how can you effectively communicate your results to different stakeholder groups?"

10. **Future Research Trajectory**: "Based on your completed dissertation, outline your future research trajectory. How will you build on these findings to develop a sustained research program in **[INSERT TOPIC]**?"

Chapter 4
75 Dissertation Research AI Prompts
Tennessee State University Specific Requirements Formatting and Style Compliance

Based on TSU Formatting Guidelines and ETD Checklist Requirements

Chapter 4: 75 Dissertation Research AI Prompts - Tennessee State University Specific Requirements, Formatting and Style Compliance

This specialized chapter provides institution-specific prompts tailored to Tennessee State University's unique dissertation requirements, formatting standards, and style guidelines. The prompts address TSU's particular academic protocols, citation requirements, structural specifications, and compliance standards that students must meet for successful dissertation completion. This chapter ensures that TSU doctoral students can navigate their institution's specific requirements while maintaining academic excellence, making it an essential resource for students pursuing advanced degrees at this particular university.

Formatting and Style Compliance

Font and Formatting Standards:
- Times New Roman 12pt, Arial 11pt, or Georgia 11pt
- Double spacing with 1 space after punctuation
- Digital copy: 1-inch margins all sides
- Bound copy: 1.5-inch left margin, 1-inch other margins
- Page numbering starting with "1" on title page, continuing through all pages.

Title Page Requirements:
- Title centered, bold, title case (maximum 12 words)
- 2 inches from top of page
- Include graduation month/year (May, August, December)
- Running head maximum 50 characters, all caps, flush left
- Keywords: italicized, maximum 5 words, title case

Required Components:
- Abstract: maximum 250 words, past tense, no indentations
- Committee page with member names and Graduate Dean signature

- Five chapters: Introduction, Literature Review, Methodology, Findings, Conclusion
- References conforming to APA 7th, MLA 9th, IEEE, or ACS
- Appendices including IRB approval, CITI certificate, instruments, letters
- Electronic Thesis & Dissertation Checklist completion

Academic Quality Standards

Source Requirements:
- Minimum 50 peer-reviewed empirical research articles
- 75% of sources within last 5 years
- Maximum 10 scholarly books and 5 dissertations
- Accurate APA formatting for all citations
- Every citation matched with reference entry.

Committee and Defense Process:
- Chair must verify originality using Turnitin/Grammarly
- Three-week manuscript distribution before defense
- Committee signatures required on defense form.
- ProQuest ETD portal submission required.
- Electronic submission checklist completion mandatory

How to Use These TSU-Specific Prompts
For Doctoral Students:
- Replace **[INSERT TOPIC]** with your specific research area.
- Use prompts sequentially following TSU's five-chapter structure.
- Ensure all responses meet TSU's specific formatting requirements.
- Complete Electronic Thesis & Dissertation Checklist using relevant prompts.

For Committee Chairs:
- Use prompts to guide student development at each chapter stage.

Chapter 1: Introduction to the Study (15 prompts)

Abstract and Problem Statement Development

1. **TSU Abstract Construction**: "Create a 250-word abstract for **[INSERT TOPIC]** following TSU requirements: purpose, theoretical foundation, research questions in narrative format, sample, location, methodology, design, data analysis, and results. Write in past tense, single paragraph, no indentations, with keywords listed separately."

2. **Problem Statement Precision**: "Develop a problem statement for **[INSERT TOPIC]** that begins with 'It is not known if and to what degree/extent...' (quantitative) or 'It is not known how or why...' (qualitative). Identify the affected population and explain contribution to solving the problem (minimum 3-4 paragraphs)."

3. **Background Study Development**: "Create a background section for **[INSERT TOPIC]** explaining both historical and present state of the problem. Identify the specific 'gap' or 'need' based on current literature summary and discuss how your study addresses this gap (minimum 2-3 paragraphs)."

Purpose and Research Questions Alignment

4. **Purpose Statement Framework**: "Craft a declarative purpose statement: 'The purpose of this study is...' that identifies research methodology (quantitative/qualitative/mixed), specific design, target population, geographic location, and variables or phenomena to be studied."

5. **Research Questions Hierarchy**: "Develop research questions that narrow the study focus and address the problem statement.

For quantitative studies, include corresponding hypotheses. Ensure questions relate directly to the problem statement and explain data collection approaches."

6. **Advancing Scientific Knowledge**: "Articulate how your **[INSERT TOPIC]** research advances scientific knowledge. Identify the specific 'gap' or 'need' from literature, describe study contribution to existing knowledge, and connect to theoretical foundations or conceptual frameworks."

Significance and Theoretical Foundations

7. **Significance Triangulation**: "Describe study significance from three required perspectives: (1) academic research contribution to the field, (2) practical contribution to practice, and (3) value added to population, community, or society."

8. **Theoretical Foundation Integration**: "Identify theory(ies) or model(s) providing study foundation from seminal sources. Connect study directly to theory and describe how research will add to or extend the theoretical framework."

9. **Methodology Justification with Citations**: "Justify your selected methodology (quantitative/qualitative/mixed) using seminal authoritative sources (not introductory textbooks). Explain why this methodology is superior to alternatives for addressing research questions."

Research Design and Operational Framework

10. **Research Design Specification**: "Describe your specific research design, explain why it's optimal compared to other designs, and briefly outline target population, sample, data collection procedures, and instruments needed to answer research questions."

11. **Operational Definitions with Citations**: "Provide precise operational definitions for all key terms, variables (quantitative), or phenomena (qualitative) that may be unknown to lay persons. Support each definition with scholarly citations."

12. **Assumptions and Limitations Framework**: "Identify methodological, theoretical, and topic-specific assumptions with rationales. Specify study limitations and delimitations, explaining their potential impact on findings (minimum 3-4

paragraphs)."

Chapter Organization and Academic Integrity

13. **Ten Strategic Points Alignment**: "Demonstrate alignment between problem statement, purpose, research questions, methodology, design, instrumentation, data collection, and analysis. How do all elements create a coherent research framework?"

14. **Chapter Summary with Citations**: "Summarize Chapter 1 key points with supporting scholarly citations. Provide transition discussion to Chapter 2 and include timeline for research completion (for proposals)."

15. **Academic Integrity Verification**: "Ensure all Chapter 1 research is scholarly, topic-related, and from highly respected academic sources. Verify in-text citations are accurate and include sources within the last 5 years (75% requirement)."

Chapter 2: Literature Review (20 prompts)

Literature Review Structure and Search Strategy

1. **30-Page Literature Review Framework**: "Design a comprehensive 30+ page literature review for **[INSERT TOPIC]**. What major themes, theoretical foundations, methodology discussions, and instrumentation sections will provide logical organization meeting TSU requirements?"

2. **Search Strategy Documentation**: "Document your systematic literature search for **[INSERT TOPIC]** including specific databases used, search terms employed, and thoroughness evaluation criteria. How does this demonstrate comprehensive coverage?"

3. **50+ Empirical Source Integration**: "Plan integration of minimum 50 peer-reviewed empirical research articles for **[INSERT TOPIC]**. How will you ensure 75% of sources are within the last 5 years while including necessary seminal works?"

Theoretical Foundations and Conceptual Framework

4. **Seminal Source Theoretical Analysis**: "Identify and analyze theory(ies) or model(s) from original seminal sources that provide reasonable conceptual framework for **[INSERT TOPIC]**. Accurately cite appropriate seminal sources for each theory."

5. **Theory-Research Question Alignment**: "Build logical argument connecting theoretical foundation to research questions. How does the theoretical framework directly inform variable identification (quantitative) or phenomena exploration (qualitative)?"

6. **Deep Historical Understanding**: "Demonstrate deep understanding of foundational, historical research relevant to your theoretical framework. How has the theoretical landscape evolved and influenced current understanding?"

Variable and Phenomena Literature Synthesis

7. **Variable Literature Mapping**: "For quantitative studies: Describe each research variable discussing prior empirical research

on variables and their relationships. Include actual data and synthesis, not just summaries."

8. **Phenomena Literature Exploration**: "For qualitative studies: Describe phenomena to be explored, discussing prior empirical research investigating similar phenomena. Include actual findings and synthesis."

9. **Theme Development with Integration**: "Structure literature review into logical themes/topics. For each major section, include: (1) introductory paragraph explaining relevance to study, (2) synthesis comparing/contrasting perspectives, (3) summary paragraph synthesizing themes."

Methodology and Instrumentation Literature

10. **Methodology Literature Synthesis**: "Analyze various methodologies and designs used in prior **[INSERT TOPIC]** research using authoritative sources. Compare strengths, limitations, and appropriateness for different research questions."

11. **Instrumentation Literature Justification**: "Provide discussion and justification for selected instrumentation based on literature

review. Argue appropriateness of chosen instruments compared to alternatives used in prior research."

12. **Research Quality Assessment**: "Evaluate quality and rigor of **[INSERT TOPIC]** studies in your review. What criteria distinguish high-quality research, and how do current studies measure against these standards?"

Source Quality and Citation Management

13. **Source Range and Quality**: "Ensure literature review includes founding theorists, peer-reviewed empirical studies, and government/foundation reports. Avoid overuse of books (maximum 10) and dissertations (maximum 5)."

14. **Citation Accuracy Verification**: "Verify that every in-text citation has corresponding reference entry and vice versa. Ensure all citations follow APA 7th edition formatting accurately."

15. **Scholarly Source Validation**: "Confirm 75% of references are scholarly sources within last 5 years (from proposal/dissertation defense date). Avoid websites, dictionaries, and undated

sources."

Literature Integration and Gap Analysis

16. **Cross-Study Pattern Analysis**: "Identify patterns, trends, and consistent findings across multiple **[INSERT TOPIC]** studies. Where do inconsistencies exist that require further investigation?"

17. **Research Gap Articulation**: "Clearly articulate specific gaps in **[INSERT TOPIC]** literature that justify your study. How do these gaps connect to your problem statement and research questions?"

18. **Empirical Evidence Integration**: "Synthesize empirical findings using actual data from reviewed studies. Structure content logically with accurate synthesis of results, not just literature summaries."

Literature Review Summary and Transition

19. **Comprehensive Literature Synthesis**: "Synthesize information from all literature review sections to define key strategic points for research. How does the review build argument for your study's value?"

20. **Chapter 2 Summary and Transition**: "Summarize gaps and needs from background/introduction, identify theories/models informing research questions, justify design/variables/instruments/population, and transition to Chapter 3."

Chapter 3: Methodology (20 prompts)

Research Philosophy and Design Justification

1. **Methodology Elaboration with Empirical Support**: "Elaborate on research methodology using empirical literature support. Provide detailed rationale why this methodology is superior to alternatives, avoiding introductory textbooks as justification sources."

2. **Research Design Optimization**: "Justify specific research design using authoritative sources. Explain how this design optimally collects data needed to answer research questions compared to alternative approaches."

3. **Ten Strategic Points Integration**: "Demonstrate how methodology chapter

integrates with and expands Chapters 1-2. Show alignment among problem statement, research questions, methodology, design, instrumentation, and analysis."

Population and Sampling Framework

4. **Population Definition Hierarchy**: "Define general population, target population, and study sample for **[INSERT TOPIC]**. Describe geographic specifics, demographics, and selection criteria creating well-defined sampling frame."

5. **Sample Size Requirements**: "Justify sample size based on research design and empirical literature. Meet TSU requirements: quantitative minimum 50 cases or 40 per cell; qualitative adequate for saturation with justification."

6. **Sampling Procedure Design**: "Design and justify sampling procedures (convenience, purposive, random, etc.) using scholarly sources. Include participant recruitment, selection, assignment processes while minimizing bias."

Data Collection and Instrumentation

7. **Instrumentation Validation**: "Provide detailed instrumentation discussion including validity and reliability from original sources. Describe instrument structure, data types, and validation evidence with citations."

8. **Data Collection Protocol**: "Detail data collection procedures allowing replication by another researcher. Include step-by-step processes, timing, participant interactions, and quality control measures."

9. **IRB and Ethical Framework**: "Address ethical considerations and IRB approval process. Discuss informed consent, potential risks/benefits, confidentiality measures, and vulnerable population protection."

Data Analysis Planning

10. **Analysis Procedures by Research Question**: "Describe detailed data analysis procedures organized by research question. For quantitative: justify statistical tests, significance levels, assumption testing. For qualitative: detail coding and theme

development."

11. **Statistical Analysis Alignment**: "For quantitative studies: Justify statistical analysis choices, demonstrate alignment with research design and data types. Include power analysis and assumption testing procedures."

12. **Qualitative Analysis Rigor**: "For qualitative studies: Provide evidence of qualitative data analysis rigor including coding process, inter-rater reliability, validity strategies, and trustworthiness establishment."

Data Management and Quality Control

13. **Comprehensive Data Management**: "Develop detailed data management procedures for collection and storage. Address security, confidentiality, retention periods, disposal methods for both paper and electronic data."

14. **Site Authorization and Access**: "Describe site authorization process, confidentiality measures, study participation requirements, and geographic specifics. Include permission letters and institutional

agreements."

15. **Reliability and Validity Evidence**: "Provide specific reliability statistics for quantitative instruments. For qualitative approaches, describe validity strategies including expert panels, member checking, and triangulation methods."

Limitations and Quality Assurance

16. **Limitation and Delimitation Analysis**: "Identify limitations related to methodology, sample, instrumentation, data collection, and analysis. Explain why limitations are unavoidable and strategies to minimize negative consequences."

17. **Quality Control Implementation**: "Describe strategies to minimize and mitigate negative consequences of limitations and delimitations. How will you ensure data quality and consistency throughout the research process?"

18. **Methodological Coherence**: "Present alignment of ten strategic points illustrating how research questions align with problem statement, methodology, design, instrumentation, data collection, and

analysis procedures."

Chapter Integration and Summary

19. **Chapter 3 Summary with Citations**: "Summarize key Chapter 3 points using authoritative, empirical sources. Demonstrate in-depth understanding of research methodology, design, and analysis techniques."

20. **Transition to Chapter 4**: "End Chapter 3 with transition discussion to Chapter 4 focus. How does methodology prepare readers for data analysis and results presentation?"

Chapter 4: Data Analysis and Results (10 prompts)

Results Organization and Presentation

1. **Research Question Organization**: "Organize Chapter 4 results by research question or hypothesis. Present findings in clear, non-evaluative manner directly addressing each research question with appropriate statistical or thematic organization."

2. **Descriptive Data Presentation**: "Provide comprehensive narrative summary of population/sample characteristics and demographics. Use visual organizers (tables, histograms, graphs) to effectively organize and display descriptive data."

3. **Statistical Results Documentation**: "For quantitative studies: Report results in appropriate statistical format including test statistics, p-values, effect sizes. Include tests of assumptions, power analysis, and control variable analysis as appropriate."

4. **Qualitative Findings Integration**: "For qualitative studies: Present analysis results in appropriate narrative format with supporting quotes and examples. Include evidence of coding process and theme development in appendices."

Data Analysis Procedures and Quality

5. **Analysis Process Documentation**: "Detail data analysis procedures used, including any deviations from Chapter 3 plans. If procedures differ from approved methods, explain and justify

changes with supporting rationale."

6. **Data Quality and Reliability**: "Assess data quality, reliability, and validity in statistical terms (quantitative) or trustworthiness approaches (qualitative). Identify sources of error, missing data, outliers, and potential effects."

7. **Sufficient Data Evidence**: "Demonstrate sufficient quantity and quality of data appropriate to research design for answering research questions. Provide evidence in chapter text or appendices supporting data adequacy."

Visual Data Presentation

8. **Graphic Organizer Optimization**: "Create appropriate graphic organizers (tables, charts, graphs, figures) to display data effectively. Ensure visual elements enhance narrative understanding and follow APA formatting requirements."

9. **Results Summary and Factual Separation**: "Provide clear, logical data summary separating factual information from interpretation. Summarize statistical data (quantitative) or analysis results (qualitative) in relation to

research questions."

Limitations and Chapter Transition

10. **Emergent Limitations Discussion**: "Discuss limitations that emerged during data analysis and how they affect result interpretation. Add data limitations to Chapters 1, 3, and 5 as appropriate with impact discussion."

Chapter 5: Summary, Conclusions, and Recommendations (10 prompts)

Study Integration and Synthesis

1. **Comprehensive Study Summary**: "Provide comprehensive summary of entire study including problem, purpose, research questions, and methodology. Remind readers of study importance and contribution to topic understanding."

2. **Findings and Literature Integration**: "Organize Chapter 5 using same section titles as Chapter 4. Compare, contrast, and synthesize study findings with Chapter 2 literature, showing alignment with or advancement of existing research."

3. **Theoretical Framework Reflection**: "Provide retrospective examination of Chapter 2 theoretical framework in light of dissertation findings. How do results advance theoretical understanding and connect back to conceptual foundations?"

Implications and Applications

4. **Theoretical and Practical Implications**: "Connect findings to theoretical framework

and prior research. Develop practical implications identifying who benefits from results and how findings can be implemented in work/educational settings."

5. **Significance Realization**: "Relate findings directly to Chapter 1 Significance of Study and Advancing Scientific Knowledge sections. How did your study achieve its intended significance and contribution?"

6. **Strengths and Weaknesses Analysis**: "Critically evaluate study strengths and weaknesses, assessing credibility of conclusions given methodological choices. Discuss degree to which conclusions are credible and bounded by research design."

Recommendations and Future Directions

7. **Future Research Recommendations**: "Provide 4-6 specific recommendations for future research relating back to study significance and Chapter 2 theoretical foundations. Identify areas needing further examination or addressing new research needs."

8. **Practice Recommendations**: "List 2-5 recommendations for future practice based on study results. Discuss who will benefit

from implementing results and practical ideas for work/educational settings implementation."

9. **Research Dissemination Strategy**: "Develop strategy for sharing research findings with appropriate audiences. How can study results reach practitioners, policymakers, and other stakeholders who could benefit from the research?"

10. **Future Research Trajectory**: "Based on completed study, outline future research directions building on current findings. How can this research contribute to sustained investigation in **[INSERT TOPIC]** area?"

Chapter 5
75 IRB Process AI Prompts

Based on TSU IRB Forms, Exempt Checklist, and Informed Consent Templates

Chapter 5: 75 IRB Process AI Prompts

This essential chapter provides comprehensive AI prompts specifically designed to navigate the Institutional Review Board (IRB) approval process, a critical requirement for research involving human subjects. The prompts guide researchers through every stage of IRB compliance, from initial protocol development and ethical considerations assessment to informed consent document creation and risk mitigation strategies. These specialized prompts help researchers understand regulatory requirements, craft compelling research justifications, address potential ethical concerns, and prepare thorough IRB applications that meet institutional and federal standards. This chapter is indispensable for doctoral students and researchers whose studies involve human participants, ensuring they can successfully obtain necessary ethical approvals while maintaining the highest standards of research integrity and participant protection.

How to Use These TSU IRB Prompts

For Principal Investigators:

- **Pre-Submission Planning**: Use prompts 1-15 to determine appropriate IRB category and review type

- **Application Development**: Apply prompts 46-60 for comprehensive application preparation

- **Consent Form Creation**: Utilize prompts 16-30 for compliant informed consent development

- **Protocol Design**: Implement prompts 31-45 for ethical research design.

For Research Teams:

- **Training Preparation**: Use prompts to understand IRB requirements before CITI training

- **Role Clarification**: Apply prompts to understand individual responsibilities in IRB process

- **Document Review**: Utilize prompts for quality assurance before submission.

For Students:

- **Dissertation Research**: Integrate IRB prompts with dissertation planning early in process

- **Thesis Development**: Use prompts for masters-level research planning and implementation

- **Learning Objectives**: Apply prompts to understand ethical research principles.

Best Practices:

- Start IRB process early in research planning phase.
- Use prompts systematically to address all requirements.
- Maintain documentation throughout research process.
- Seek guidance from IRB office when uncertain about requirements.
- Update protocols promptly when research changes occur.

These prompts ensure compliance with Tennessee State University's IRB requirements while supporting high-quality, ethical research across all disciplines.

IRB Determination and Classification (15 prompts)

IRB Type Assessment

1. **IRB Category Determination**: "Analyze my **[topic]** research involving **[participants/data type]** to determine if it qualifies for Exempt, Expedited, or Full Review. Consider the six exemption categories: educational settings, surveys/interviews, public officials, existing data, public benefit programs, and food studies."

2. **Exempt Category Analysis**: "Evaluate my research design for **[topic]** against TSU's exemption checklist. Does it meet Category **[1-6]** requirements? Address all true/false statements for the relevant category including prisoner exclusion and FDA regulation requirements."

3. **Educational Setting Exemption**: "Determine if my **[educational research topic]** qualifies for Category 1 exemption. Will research be conducted in established educational settings using normal educational practices without involving

prisoners or FDA-regulated materials?"

4. **Survey/Interview Exemption**: "Assess whether **my [survey/interview study]** meets Category 2 exemption criteria. Can participants be identified from responses? Could disclosure reasonably place subjects at risk of criminal/civil liability or damage their reputation?"

5. **Existing Data Exemption**: "Evaluate my **[secondary data analysis]** for Category 4 exemption. Is the data existing before IRB proposal submission? Are sources publicly available OR will information be recorded so participants cannot be identified?"

Risk Assessment and Ethical Standards

6. **Minimal Risk Evaluation**: "Assess whether my **[topic]** research presents more than minimal risk to participants. Consider physical, psychological, social, economic, and legal risks compared to everyday life activities."

7. **Vulnerable Population Analysis**: "Determine if my research involves vulnerable populations (children, pregnant women, prisoners, cognitive impairment, students in my classes). What additional

protections are required for **[specific population]**?"

8. **Privacy and Confidentiality Framework**: "Design privacy and confidentiality protections for my **[topic]** research. How will I protect participant identity, secure data storage, limit access, and handle potential breaches?"

9. **Equitable Subject Selection**: "Ensure equitable subject selection for **[topic]** research. How will recruitment avoid coercion and fairly distribute risks/benefits across demographic groups?"

10. **TSU Ethical Standards Compliance**: "Verify my research meets TSU ethical standards: minimal risk, equitable selection, adequate confidentiality provisions, appropriate consent process, and privacy protection."

Federal Regulation Compliance

11. **FDA Regulation Assessment**: "Determine if my **[research involving drugs/devices/biologics]** is subject to FDA regulations. Does this disqualify exemption and require full IRB review?"

12. **Prisoner Research Exclusion**: "Confirm my research excludes known prisoners as participants. If prisoners might be included, what additional protections and oversight are required?"

13. **Federal Statute Compliance**: "For public benefit program research, identify relevant federal statutes requiring confidentiality protection. How do these requirements affect exemption eligibility?"

14. **Emergency Use Evaluation**: "Assess if my research involves emergency use of unapproved test articles. What reporting requirements exist within five business days to TSU IRB?"

15. **Research Definition Compliance**: "Verify my activity meets DHHS definition of 'research' as systematic investigation designed to develop generalizable knowledge. Does my [project type] qualify as research requiring IRB review?"

Informed Consent Development (15 prompts)

Consent Form Structure and Content

1. **Informed Consent Introduction**: "Draft an introduction section **for [project title]** informed consent explaining the college/department's commitment to human subject's protection, voluntary participation, and withdrawal rights without consequences."

2. **Purpose Statement Creation**: "Write a clear purpose statement for **[research topic]** informed consent. Explain the study purpose in accessible language and emphasize voluntary participation not required for course grades or program completion."

3. **Procedure Description**: "Describe expected participant tasks for **[research activities]** in informed consent. Include total anticipated participation time and step-by-step procedure explanations participants can understand."

4. **Risk Disclosure Framework**: "Develop risk disclosure section for **[research type]**. Address anticipated minimal risks or state 'There are no anticipated risks in completing this [survey/questionnaire/interview, etc.]' if

appropriate."

5. **Benefits and Compensation Statement**: "Create benefits and compensation section clarifying no individual benefits or financial compensation, but noting any provided items (food, handouts) participants will receive."

Confidentiality and Privacy Protection

6. **Confidentiality Statement Development**: "Write participant confidentiality section using IRB application language regarding personal identifying information protection and security processes for data handling and storage."

7. **Data Security Procedures**: "Detail data security procedures for **[data type]** including collection methods, storage locations, access limitations, encryption requirements, and retention/disposal timelines."

8. **Identifiable Information Handling**: "Explain how identifiable information will be handled throughout **[research process]**. Address direct identifiers, indirect identifiers, coding systems, and re-

identification risks."

9. **Data Sharing and Publication**: "Describe how participant data may be used in publications, presentations, or shared with other researchers while maintaining confidentiality protections."

10. **Breach Response Protocol**: "Develop protocol for responding to potential confidentiality breaches including notification procedures, mitigation strategies, and participant communication plans."

Consent Process and Documentation

11. **Refusal to Sign Rights**: "Clarify participant rights to refuse consent signing without affecting their access to Tennessee State University programs, events, or services they are receiving."

12. **Withdrawal Process**: "Explain participant withdrawal procedures including timeline for data destruction, process for withdrawing identifiable data, and researcher contact information for questions or consent cancellation."

13. **Age and Eligibility Verification**: "Design age verification and eligibility criteria section confirming participants are at least 18 years old and meet [specific population criteria] for study participation."

14. **Contact Information Requirements**: "Provide researcher contact information for questions, concerns, or consent withdrawal including **[researcher name and email]** and IRB contact for complaints or concerns."

15. **Electronic Consent Considerations**: "Adapt informed consent for electronic distribution and completion. Address digital signature requirements, consent form access, and participant copy provision."

Research Design and Protocol Development (15 prompts)

Study Design Documentation

1. **Research Question Alignment**: "Align research questions with IRB requirements for **[topic]**. Ensure questions address systematic investigation designed to develop generalizable knowledge while maintaining ethical standards."

2. **Participant Recruitment Strategy**: "Design ethical recruitment strategy for **[target population]**. Address recruitment methods, materials, incentives, avoiding coercion, and ensuring voluntary participation."

3. **Inclusion/Exclusion Criteria**: "Develop clear inclusion/exclusion criteria for **[research population]**. Ensure criteria are scientifically justified, ethically appropriate, and don't unfairly exclude groups."

4. **Data Collection Procedures**: "Detail step-by-step data collection procedures for **[research method]**. Include participant interactions, data recording methods, quality control measures, and timeline."

5. **Sample Size Justification**: "Justify sample size for [research design] balancing scientific validity with minimal participant burden. Address power analysis (quantitative) or saturation rationale (qualitative)."

Instrumentation and Materials

6. **Survey Instrument Validation**: "Document validation and reliability of **[survey instruments]**. Include psychometric

properties, pilot testing results, and appropriateness for target population."

7. **Interview Protocol Development**: "Develop structured interview protocol for **[research topic]**. Include question sequencing, probes, sensitive topic handling, and interviewer training requirements."

8. **Observation Protocol Design**: "Create observation protocol for **[behavioral research]**. Address observer training, structured observation forms, inter-rater reliability, and participant awareness."

9. **Recruitment Materials Review**: "Design recruitment materials (flyers, emails, announcements) that accurately represent research without coercion. Ensure IRB approval before distribution."

10. **Data Use Agreements**: "Develop data use agreements for multi-site research or secondary data access. Address data sharing permissions, security requirements, and publication rights."

Risk Mitigation and Safety

11. **Psychological Risk Mitigation**: "Develop procedures for addressing psychological

distress during **[sensitive research topic]**. Include referral resources, stopping criteria, and follow-up procedures."

12. **Physical Safety Protocols**: "Design physical safety protocols for **[research setting]**. Address emergency procedures, safety equipment, participant screening, and researcher training."

13. **Social Risk Management**: "Address potential social risks from research participation including stigma, relationship impacts, or community consequences. Develop mitigation strategies."

14. **Economic Risk Consideration**: "Evaluate potential economic risks to participants including time costs, transportation expenses, or impact on employment/benefits."

15. **Legal Risk Assessment**: "Assess potential legal risks from research participation including mandatory reporting requirements, disclosure obligations, and liability protections.".

IRB Submission and Documentation (15 prompts)

Application Completion

1. **PI Information Compilation**: "Compile Principal Investigator information including name, department, email, phone, university affiliation, and qualifications for conducting proposed research."

2. **Research Team Documentation**: "Document all research team members including additional researchers, their roles, qualifications, and CITI training completion status."

3. **CITI Training Verification**: "Verify all research team members have completed appropriate CITI training modules. Upload certificates and ensure currency of training."

4. **Institutional Collaboration**: "Document collaborating institutions and their IRB approvals. Address data sharing agreements, oversight responsibilities, and approval coordination."

5. **Amendment Documentation**: "Prepare amendment documentation for changes to approved research including modified

procedures, new instruments, additional sites, or personnel changes."

Supporting Documentation

6. **Research Proposal Integration**: "Integrate research proposal with IRB application ensuring consistency between scientific aims and ethical considerations across all documents."

7. **Grant Proposal Alignment**: "Align IRB application with grant proposal requirements ensuring ethical considerations match funding agency expectations and requirements."

8. **Institutional Requirements**: "Address institutional-specific requirements including departmental approvals, facility use permissions, and administrative clearances."

9. **Professional Standards**: "Ensure research design meets professional standards for **[discipline]** including methodological rigor, ethical guidelines, and publication standards."

10. **Quality Assurance**: "Implement quality assurance procedures for IRB documentation including accuracy checks,

completeness verification, and deadline management."

Review Process Navigation

11. **Pre-Submission Review**: "Conduct pre-submission review of IRB application including completeness check, document alignment, and anticipated reviewer questions."

12. **Response to IRB Feedback**: "Develop systematic approach for responding to IRB feedback including requested modifications, clarifications, and additional documentation."

13. **Approval Implementation**: "Plan implementation procedures following IRB approval including researcher training, participant recruitment initiation, and data collection commencement."

14. **Continuing Review Preparation**: "Prepare for continuing review requirements including progress reports, adverse event reporting, and protocol modification procedures."

15. **Close-Out Procedures**: "Plan research close-out procedures including final reports,

data retention/destruction plans, and participant debriefing requirements."

Data Management and Analysis (10 prompts)

Data Handling Protocols

1. **Data Collection Security**: "Design secure data collection procedures for **[data type]** including electronic safeguards, physical security measures, and access controls."

2. **Data Storage and Retention**: "Develop data storage and retention plan addressing storage locations, backup procedures, retention timeline, and secure disposal methods."

3. **Data De-identification**: "Create data de-identification procedures removing direct and indirect identifiers while maintaining data utility for analysis purposes."

4. **Access Control Management**: "Design access control procedures limiting data access to authorized personnel with appropriate training and confidentiality agreements."

5. **Data Monitoring Procedures**: "Implement data monitoring procedures for quality

control, security compliance, and adverse event detection throughout research duration."

Analysis and Reporting

6. **Analysis Plan Documentation**: "Document analysis plan ensuring analytical approaches align with research questions while protecting participant confidentiality in results reporting."

7. **Results Reporting Standards**: "Develop results reporting standards ensuring participant confidentiality in publications, presentations, and reports while accurately representing findings."

8. **Adverse Event Reporting**: "Establish adverse event reporting procedures including identification criteria, notification timelines, and IRB communication requirements."

9. **Data Sharing Protocols**: "Design data sharing protocols for collaborative research or public data repositories ensuring participant consent and confidentiality protection."

10. **Publication Ethics**: "Address publication ethics including authorship criteria, data ownership, participant acknowledgment, and journal disclosure requirements."

Post-Approval Responsibilities (5 prompts)

Ongoing Compliance

1. **Protocol Adherence Monitoring**: "Implement procedures for monitoring protocol adherence including training updates, procedure reviews, and deviation documentation."

2. **Participant Communication**: "Design ongoing participant communication procedures including study updates, results sharing, and contact maintenance for longitudinal studies."

3. **IRB Communication**: "Establish regular IRB communication including progress reports, modification requests, adverse event notifications, and annual reviews."

4. **Regulatory Updates**: "Monitor regulatory changes affecting research including IRB policy updates, federal requirement changes, and institutional guideline modifications."

5. **Research Integrity Maintenance**: "Maintain research integrity throughout study duration including data quality assurance, ethical compliance monitoring, and professional standard adherence."

Conclusion

The integration of artificial intelligence in higher education academic writing represents more than a technological advancement; it constitutes a fundamental reimagining of how we teach, learn, and assess intellectual development in the digital age. The frameworks presented by Dr. Robbie K. Melton and Dr. Nicole Arrighi provide roadmaps for this transformation, offering structured approaches that maintain academic integrity while harnessing AI's potential for educational enhancement.

The transition from convenience-based AI use to competence-driven applications requires institutional commitment, faculty expertise, and student engagement. However, the potential benefits—enhanced critical thinking, improved research capabilities, better preparation for the digital workforce, and increased accessibility to high-quality education—far outweigh the implementation challenges.

Higher education administrators and faculty who embrace this transformation position their institutions and students for success in an AI-integrated world. Those who resist risk leaving their students unprepared for professional environments where AI literacy is not optional but essential. The question is not whether AI will transform academic writing, but whether our institutions will lead this transformation or be left behind by it.

The frameworks and strategies outlined in this paper provide a foundation for ethical, effective AI integration that enhances rather than diminishes the educational mission of higher education. By focusing on progressive skill development, ethical guidelines, and pedagogical excellence, we can ensure that AI becomes a powerful tool for intellectual growth rather than a threat to academic integrity.

The future of higher education lies not in avoiding technological innovation but in embracing it thoughtfully and strategically. The time for hesitation has passed; the time for thoughtful, ethical, and educationally sound AI integration is now. Our students, our institutions, and our society depend on our willingness to navigate this transformation with wisdom, courage, and commitment to educational excellence.

REFERENCES

Arrighi, N. (2023). *AI-C2 utilization spectrum: Five-stage learning spectrum for utilizing artificial intelligence in education.* Tennessee State University.

Bainbridge, C. (2015). AQR dissertation checklist chapters 1-5 (Version 9) [Excel spreadsheet]. Grand Canyon University. Note: This document was originally created by Cynthia Bainbridge at Grand Canyon University in 2011, with the final version (v.9) dated 2015 based on the filename.

Hassell, R. (2024). *ASCEND-AI: Elevating learning with smart AI prompts.* Tennessee State University, Smart Innovation Technology Center. https://ai-tnstatesmartcenter.org

Horton, M. (2024). *P.A.C. it up! Educational aid for artificial intelligence.* Tennessee State University, Smart Innovation Technology Center. https://ai-tnstatesmartcenter.org

Melton, R. K. (2023). *AI prompt rubric for education: The AI-PromptScale framework.* Tennessee State University Smart Center.

Tennessee State University, School of Graduate and Professional Studies. (2024). *Formatting and style guidelines for theses and dissertations* (2024-2025 ed.). Tennessee State University.

Tennessee State University, School of Graduate and Professional Studies. (2024). *Electronic thesis & dissertation checklist*. Tennessee State University.

Tennessee State University, Institutional Review Board. (2015). *2015 AQR dissertation checklist chapters 1-5* (Version 9) [Excel file]. Tennessee State University

Tennessee State University, Institutional Review Board. (n.d.). *Template letter of consent* [Word document]. Tennessee State University.

Tennessee State University, Institutional Review Board. (n.d.). *IRB exempt checklist* [Word document]. Tennessee State University.

www.ingramcontent.com/pod-product-compliance
Lightning Source LLC
Chambersburg PA
CBHW071215160426
43196CB00012B/2312